MEGA FACTS

SHARKS

AND OTHER
CREATURES
OF THE DEEP

THIS BOOK BELONGS TO
GIOVANNI

make believe ideas

CONTENTS

UNDER THE SEA

The Earth's oceans are filled with MILLIONS of plants and animals.

rays

eels

fish

octopuses

whales

Look through this mini book to find MEGA facts about sharks and other cool creatures of the deep!

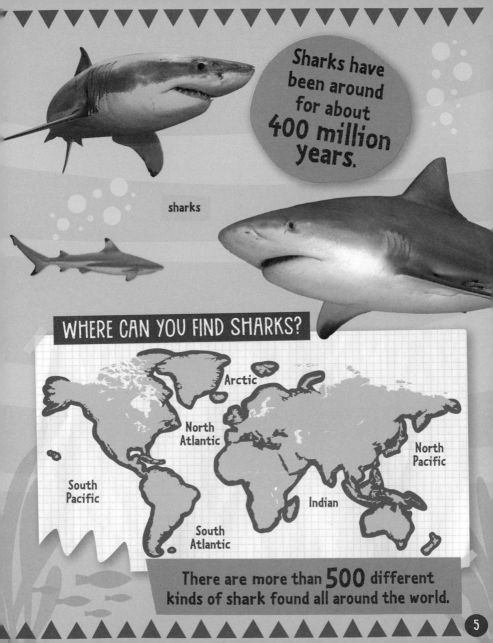

Sharks have been around for about **400 million years**.

sharks

WHERE CAN YOU FIND SHARKS?

Arctic

North Atlantic

North Pacific

South Pacific

Indian

South Atlantic

There are more than **500** different kinds of shark found all around the world.

WHAT IS A SHARK?

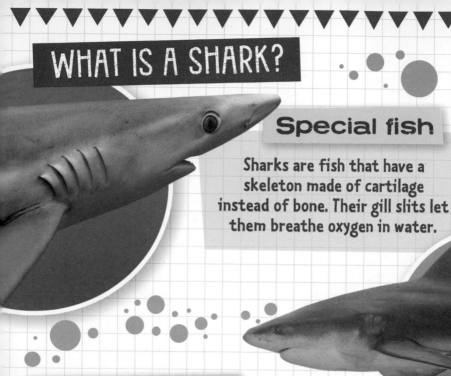

Special fish

Sharks are fish that have a skeleton made of cartilage instead of bone. Their gill slits let them breathe oxygen in water.

Never-ending teeth

Sharks have about five rows of teeth. When they lose a tooth, one from another row moves forward and replaces it.

All shapes and sizes

Sharks vary in shape and size, from the tiny dwarf lantern shark to the giant whale shark.

Topsy-turvy tail

Unlike other fish, sharks' tail fins are bigger at the top than at the bottom. This helps push them swiftly through water.

Super senses

Fine-tuned senses of hearing, smell, touch, and electroreception help these predators find food.

HOW DO BABY SHARKS SURVIVE?

Nursery

Female sharks often find a safe nursery area to give birth, such as a lagoon.

Egg or pup?

More than half of all sharks give birth to live pups. The rest lay eggs, which can take up to a year to hatch.

Baby teeth

Shark pups are born with teeth so they can hunt straight away.

Independence

Shark pups are left to look after themselves as soon as they are born.

Camouflage

To avoid being eaten by bigger sharks, some shark pups hide among their surroundings.

GREAT WHITE SHARK

Great white sharks are the LARGEST predatory shark in the oceans.

WHERE CAN YOU FIND THEM?

Arctic

North Atlantic

North Pacific

South Pacific

Indian

South Atlantic

WHAT DO THEY EAT?

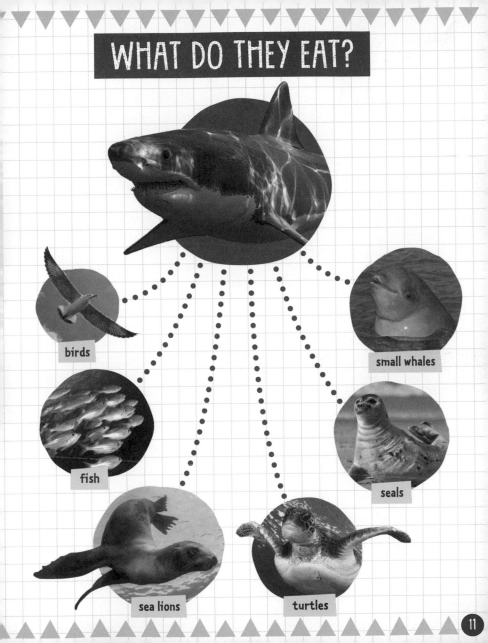

birds

small whales

fish

seals

sea lions

turtles

WHAT DOES A GREAT WHITE SHARK LOOK LIKE?

powerful tail

Weight:

up to 2,450 lbs (1,110 kg)

great white shark | rhino

white belly

Length:

up to 20 ft (6 m)

torpedo-shaped body

sharp teeth

Camouflage

Their white bellies blend in with the brighter water surface and their dark-colored back blends in with the dark water underneath.

WHAT MAKES GREAT WHITE SHARKS SUCH FIERCE PREDATORS?

Speed

They can travel through the water at more than 25 mph (40 km/h)!

Agility

Great white sharks often attack fast-moving prey from below by launching themselves out of the water. This is called breaching.

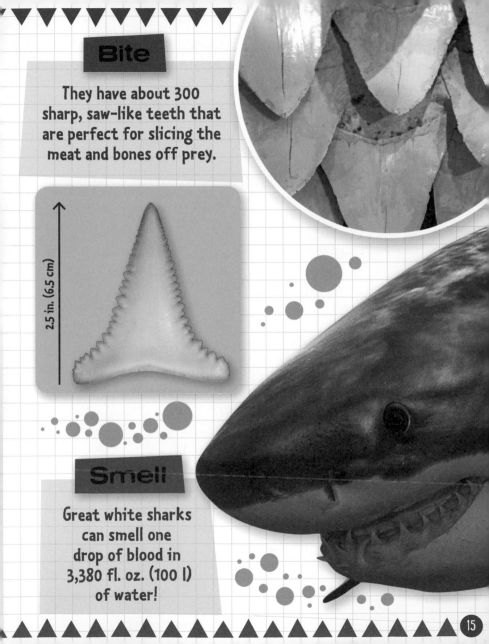

Bite

They have about 300 sharp, saw-like teeth that are perfect for slicing the meat and bones off prey.

2.5 in. (6.5 cm)

Smell

Great white sharks can smell one drop of blood in 3,380 fl. oz. (100 l) of water!

TIGER SHARK

TIGER sharks love warm waters and are found both close to shore and far out to sea.

WHERE CAN YOU FIND THEM?

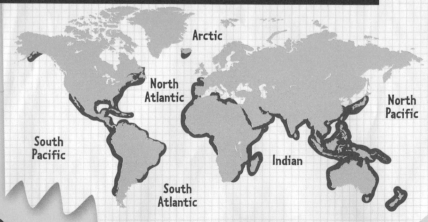

Arctic

North Atlantic

North Pacific

South Pacific

Indian

South Atlantic

WHAT DO THEY EAT?

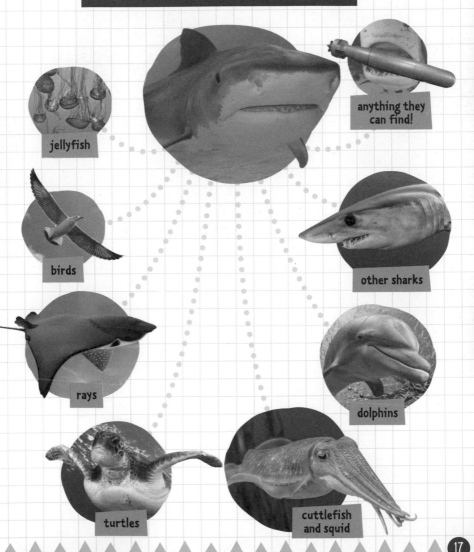

jellyfish

anything they can find!

birds

other sharks

rays

dolphins

turtles

cuttlefish and squid

WHAT DOES A
TIGER SHARK LOOK LIKE?

stripes
and spots

Weight:

up to 1,400 lbs (635 kg)

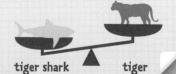

tiger shark   tiger

Length:

up to 16 ft (5 m)

saw-like
jagged teeth

powerful jaws

Tiger stripes

The tiger shark gets its name from
the striped markings on its body. As it
grows older, these stripes slowly fade.

WHY ARE TIGER SHARKS SUCH GOOD HUNTERS?

Fearless feasting

Tiger sharks are not afraid to come close to shore while hunting for food.

Strong stomach

In tiger shark stomachs, scientists have found shoes, bottles, a drum, a car license plate, and even a suit of armor!

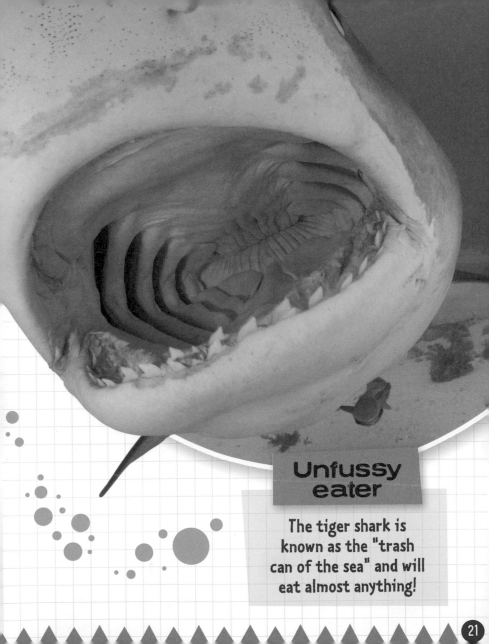

Unfussy eater

The tiger shark is known as the "trash can of the sea" and will eat almost anything!

QUIZ TIME

1 WHAT IS A BABY SHARK CALLED?

kitten ☐   calf ☐   pup ☐

2 BABY SHARKS ARE BORN WITH TEETH.

true ☐   false ☐

3 WHICH OF THE BELOW ISN'T ON A GREAT WHITE SHARK'S MENU?

hamburgers ☐

fish ☐

seals ☐

4 WHAT TYPE OF SHARK IS THIS?

....

22

5 WHEN A GREAT WHITE SHARK LAUNCHES ITSELF OUT OF THE WATER, IT IS KNOWN AS

....

6 A GREAT WHITE SHARK'S TOOTH IS BIGGER THAN...

your head. ☐   your ear. ☐   your hand. ☐

7 HOW HEAVY IS A TIGER SHARK?

lbs
....

8 CAN YOU RECOGNIZE WHAT TIGER SHARK PREY HAS BEEN PIXELATED?

....

BULL SHARK

Bull sharks can be AGGRESSIVE and have been known to head-butt their prey.

WHERE CAN YOU FIND THEM?

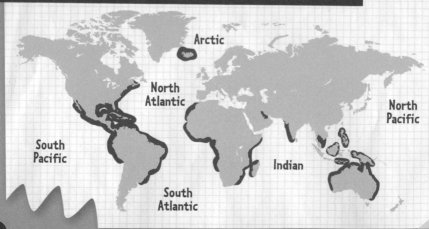

Arctic

North Atlantic

North Pacific

South Pacific

Indian

South Atlantic

WHAT DO BULL SHARKS LOOK LIKE?

Weight:

up to 500 lbs (225 kg)

bull

bull shark

thick body

short snout

Length:

up to 11 ft (3.4 m)

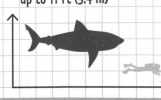

Power bite

The bull shark's wide, muscular jaws give it the most powerful bite of all sharks!

HOW DO BULL SHARKS HUNT?

Sense of smell

Bull sharks don't have very good eyesight, so they use their incredible sense of smell to detect prey.

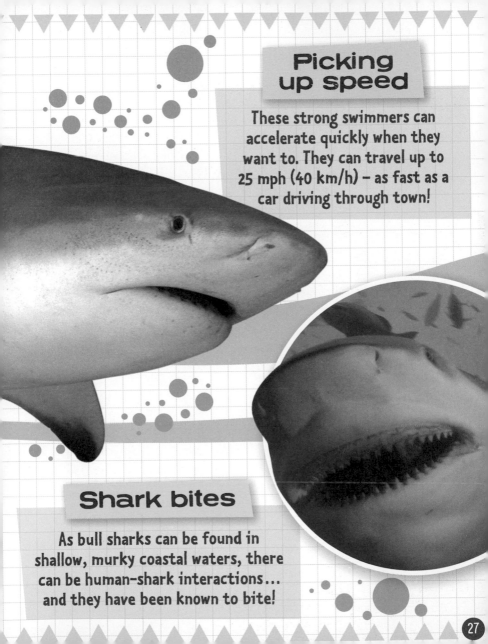

Picking up speed

These strong swimmers can accelerate quickly when they want to. They can travel up to 25 mph (40 km/h) – as fast as a car driving through town!

Shark bites

As bull sharks can be found in shallow, murky coastal waters, there can be human-shark interactions... and they have been known to bite!

WHERE DO
BULL SHARKS LIVE?

River cruising

If you are ever sailing up the Amazon River, watch out for bull sharks! They have been spotted more than 2,500 miles (4,000 km) upriver.

Freshwater explorers

Bull sharks have the amazing ability to retain salt inside their bodies, so they can survive in both freshwater rivers and salty seas.

EELS AND SEA SNAKES

Eels are long, ribbon-like fish that have fins and gills to breathe underwater.

moray eel

American eel

European eel

There are more than 800 species of eel.

conger eel

HOW ARE SEA SNAKES DIFFERENT FROM LAND SNAKES?

Sea snakes are rope-like reptiles that live mostly in coral reefs. There are more than **60 species** of sea snake!

Their tails are **paddle-shaped** to help them move through water.

They still breathe air, so they have to come to the surface **every hour.**

Almost all of sea snakes are **venomous!**

WHAT DOES A MORAY EEL LOOK LIKE?

Hide-and-eat

Morays spend much of their time hiding in caves and among rocks on the ocean floor, waiting to attack prey.

small eyes

long teeth

wide jaws

Double bite!

The moray eel has two sets of jaws that help it to bite and swallow large prey, even small sharks.

QUIZ TIME

1 HOW HEAVY IS A BULL SHARK?

.... lbs

2 WHAT GIVES A BULL SHARK ITS POWERFUL BITE?

muscular jaws ☐   sharp teeth ☐   strong tongue ☐

3 BULL SHARKS HAVE EXCELLENT EYESIGHT.

true ☐   false ☐

4 WHICH OF THE BELOW ENABLES AN EEL TO BREATHE UNDERWATER?

snorkel ☐

gills ☐

scuba gear ☐

5 WHAT TYPE OF EEL IS THIS?

....

6 MORAY EELS HAVE .... SETS OF JAWS THAT HELP THEM TO BITE AND SWALLOW LARGE PREY.

7 BULL SHARKS CAN STORE WHAT IN THEIR BODIES?

pepper ☐   salt ☐   cinnamon ☐

8 CAN YOU RECOGNIZE WHICH ANIMAL HAS BEEN PIXELATED?

....

WHALE SHARK

The whale shark is the LARGEST FISH in the ocean. It can grow as long as a school bus!

Weight:

up to 41,200 lbs (18,700 kg)

whale shark   elephant

Length:

up to 46 ft (14 m)

WHERE CAN YOU FIND THEM?

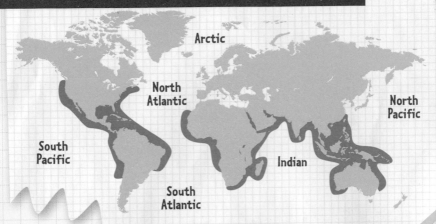

Arctic

North
Atlantic

North
Pacific

South
Pacific

Indian

South
Atlantic

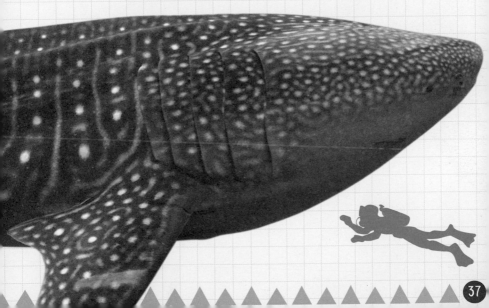

HOW DOES A WHALE SHARK EAT?

Small lunch

Krill are small, shrimp-like crustaceans that make up a big part of a whale shark's diet.

gulping water

Filter feeders

Whale sharks gulp down water and strain plankton, such as krill and fish eggs, from the water like a sieve.

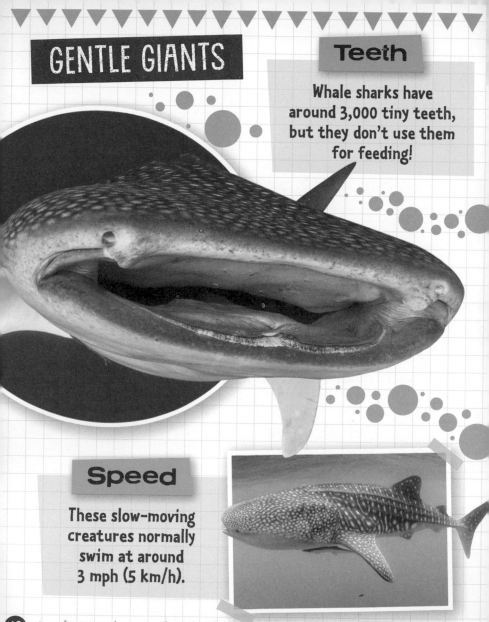

GENTLE GIANTS

Teeth

Whale sharks have around 3,000 tiny teeth, but they don't use them for feeding!

Speed

These slow-moving creatures normally swim at around 3 mph (5 km/h).

Docile

They are calm creatures who have been known to swim alongside boats and divers.

Unique

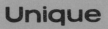

The spotted patterns on their skin is unique. This means that each whale shark pattern is different!

BASKING SHARK

Slow travelers

Basking sharks move slowly as they travel long distances in search of food and mates.

Open wide

Basking sharks are passive filter feeders. This means that they need to swim forward to scoop up food.

large body

scooping mouth

WHALE
WATCHING

Blue whale

The blue whale is the largest animal on Earth. Just its tongue can weigh as much as an elephant!

Humpback whale

Humpback whales are known for the haunting noises they make, which can travel hundreds of miles through the water.

Beluga whale

These small, white whales live mostly in the Arctic Ocean. They are able to swim backward!

Sperm whale

Sperm whales have huge heads that hold one of the biggest brains of any creature in the world!

ORCA

On the hunt

Orcas are smart and powerful predators. They hunt in groups and eat fish, birds, seals, penguins, and whales.

Did you know?

Even though they are sometimes known as killer whales, orcas aren't whales at all. They are actually the largest member of the dolphin family.

47

QUIZ TIME

1 HOW HEAVY IS A WHALE SHARK?

lbs
....

2 WHAT IS THE LARGEST ANIMAL ON EARTH?

whale shark ☐   blue whale ☐   elephant ☐

4 WHICH OF THE ANIMALS BELOW CAN SWIM BACKWARD?

beluga whale ☐

3 WHALE SHARKS ARE FILTER FEEDERS.

true ☐   false ☐

humpback whale ☐   sperm whale ☐

5 WHAT TYPE OF SHARK IS THIS?

....

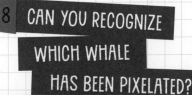

6 WHALE SHARKS HAVE AROUND 3,000 TINY

....

7 WHAT DOESN'T AN ORCA EAT?

penguins ☐

humans ☐

seals ☐

8 CAN YOU RECOGNIZE WHICH WHALE HAS BEEN PIXELATED?

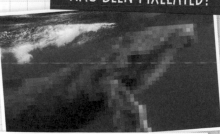

....

....

49

HAMMERHEAD
SHARK

There are eight different types of hammerhead shark.

WHERE CAN YOU FIND THEM?

Some hammerheads travel long distances in groups of up to 100 sharks, called schools, in search of cooler waters.

Arctic

North Atlantic

North Pacific

South Pacific

Indian

Different types of hammerhead can be found all over the world.

WHAT DO THEY EAT?

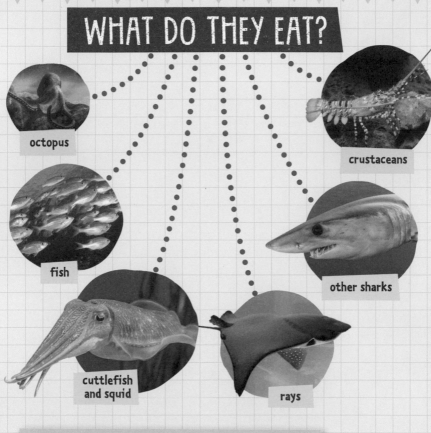

octopus

crustaceans

fish

other sharks

cuttlefish and squid

rays

Biggest vs. smallest

Great hammerhead
up to 20 ft (6 m)

Scalloped bonnethead
shark up to 36 in. (92 cm)

HOW DOES A HAMMERHEAD SHARK SENSE ITS PREY?

nostrils set
far apart

wide head

up to 1,000 lbs (450 kg)

hammerhead
shark

polar
bear

eyes on
both ends

Blind spot

A hammerhead can look up and down as
well as left and right. The only place it
can't see is right in front of its nose!

DIFFERENT HAMMERHEADS

Smooth hammerhead

This clever predator uses its smooth, wide head to pin down stingrays – its favorite food.

Scalloped hammerhead

Scalloped hammerheads communicate to other sharks within their group with a set of body movements.

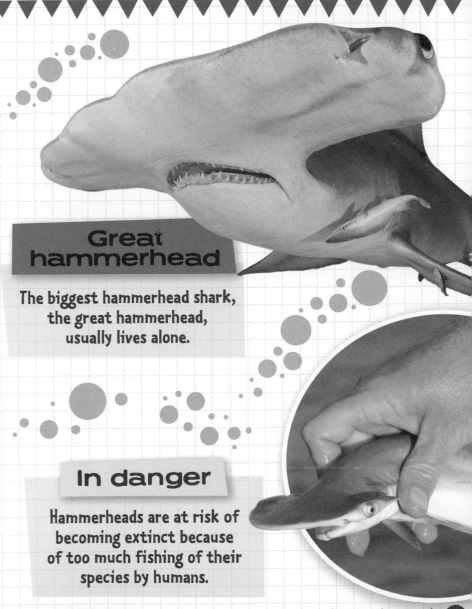

Great hammerhead

The biggest hammerhead shark, the great hammerhead, usually lives alone.

In danger

Hammerheads are at risk of becoming extinct because of too much fishing of their species by humans.

AMAZING
RAYS

Rays are closely related to sharks. They have flat bodies with tails and wide pectoral fins, which can look like wings.

Torpedo ray

Torpedo rays can produce enough electricity to produce anything up to a 200-volt shock (enough to power a TV)!

Mobula ray

These amazing rays can leap from the water and do somersaults.

Spotted eagle ray

These rays use their strong sense of smell to sniff out prey hidden under the sand.

Blue-spotted stingray

This stingray's bright blue spots warn off predators. It has two venomous spikes on the end of its tail that it uses in defense.

GIANT
MANTA RAY

long tail

Giant brains

A giant manta ray has a large brain that allows it to remember things, learn, and even recognize different objects.

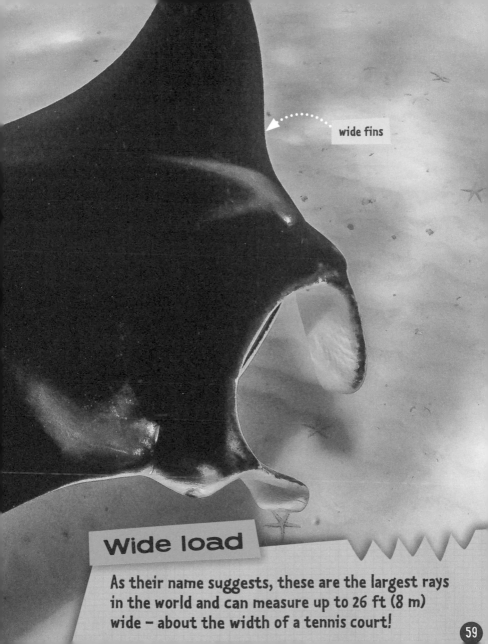

wide fins

wide load

As their name suggests, these are the largest rays in the world and can measure up to 26 ft (8 m) wide – about the width of a tennis court!

QUIZ TIME

1 HOW HEAVY IS A HAMMERHEAD SHARK?

lbs
....

2 WHICH IS THE LARGEST SPECIES OF HAMMERHEAD SHARK?

great hammerhead shark ☐

scalloped hammerhead shark ☐

smooth hammerhead shark ☐

3 MOBULA RAYS CAN'T DO SOMERSAULTS.

true ☐   false ☐

4 WHICH RAY USES ITS STRONG SENSE OF SMELL TO SNIFF OUT PREY?

torpedo ray ☐   mobula ray ☐   spotted eagle ray ☐

5 WHAT TYPE OF RAY IS THIS?

. . . .

6 THERE ARE

. . . .

DIFFERENT TYPES OF HAMMERHEAD SHARK.

7 TORPEDO RAYS CAN PRODUCE ENOUGH ELECTRICITY TO...

light a sports stadium. ☐

power a TV. ☐

8 CAN YOU RECOGNIZE WHICH RAY HAS BEEN PIXELATED?

. . . .

. . . .

WOBBEGONG
SHARK

patterned skin

frilled mouth

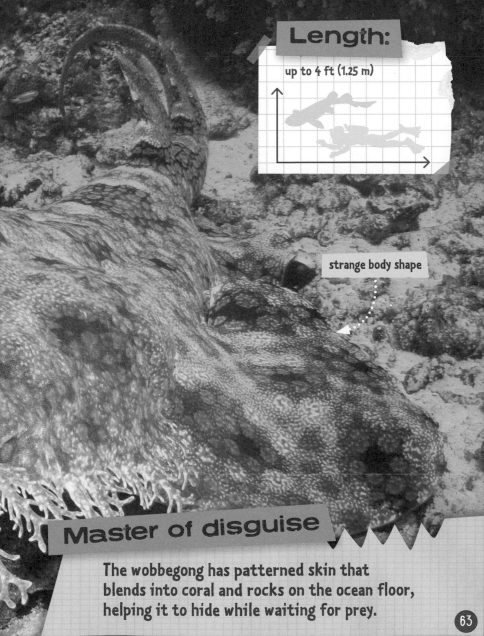

Length:

up to 4 ft (1.25 m)

strange body shape

Master of disguise

The wobbegong has patterned skin that blends into coral and rocks on the ocean floor, helping it to hide while waiting for prey.

63

HOW DOES THE WOBBEGONG ATTRACT ITS PREY?

Carpet shark

The wobbegong is a carpet shark. It lies on the ocean floor in wait, looking like a shaggy rug!

Tail trance

The wobbegong waves its tail back and forth to lure fish toward it.

Sudden strike

When they're ready to eat, these sharks open their jaws so quickly that they suck in fish whole.

What does it eat?

Wobbegongs like to eat small fish that swim by, but they also feast on crabs and octopuses.

EPAULETTE
SHARK

> The epaulette shark possesses a surprising TALENT. Turn the page to discover what it is!

WHERE CAN YOU FIND THEM?

Arctic

North Atlantic

North Pacific

South Pacific

Indian

South Atlantic

WHAT DO THEY EAT?

worms

crustaceans

Length:

up to 3.3 ft (1 m)

Weight:

up to 2 lbs (1 kg)

epaulette shark   dog

HOW DOES AN EPAULETTE SHARK LIKE TO TRAVEL?

Changing tides

As the tide goes out, the epaulette doesn't go with it. It stays to hunt around rock pools on the shoreline.

eyespots on its back to
scare away predators

strong fins used for
walking on shore

walk like a shark

Out of water, the epaulette shark
"walks" across coral and rocks using
its strong fins as "legs."

THRESHER SHARK

long tail to stun prey

Weight:

up to 750 lbs (340 kg)

thresher
shark

grizzly
bear

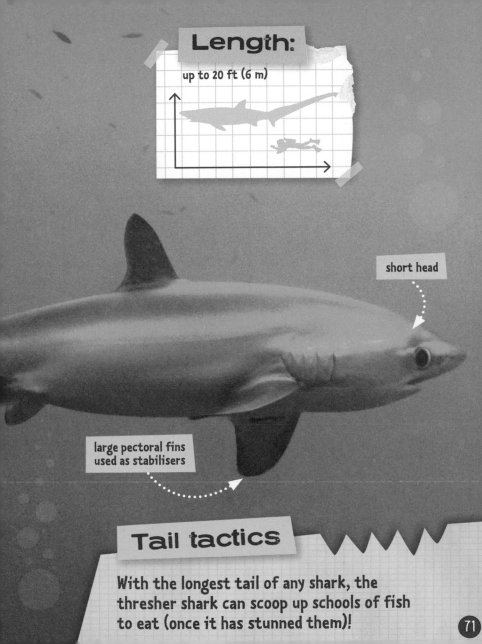

Length:

up to 20 ft (6 m)

short head

large pectoral fins
used as stabilisers

Tail tactics

With the longest tail of any shark, the
thresher shark can scoop up schools of fish
to eat (once it has stunned them)!

WHAT MAKES THE THRESHER SHARK UNIQUE?

High jump

This agile shark can jump as high as 10 ft (3 m) above water, even getting its long tail fully in the air.

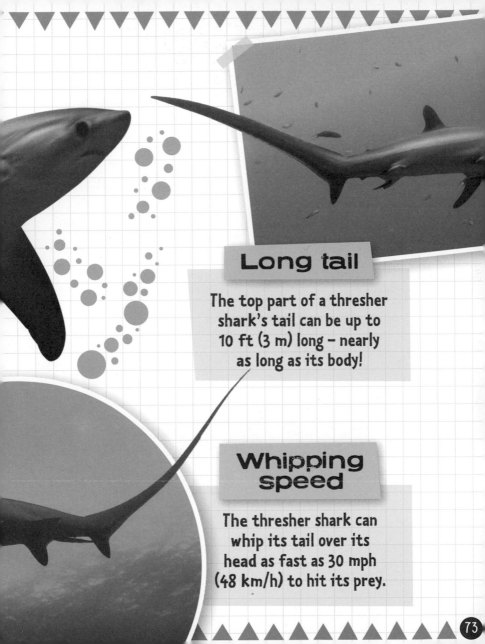

Long tail

The top part of a thresher shark's tail can be up to 10 ft (3 m) long – nearly as long as its body!

Whipping speed

The thresher shark can whip its tail over its head as fast as 30 mph (48 km/h) to hit its prey.

FASCINATING

FISH

Flying fish

These four-winged wonders swim up to 37 mph (60 km/h) to propel themselves straight into the air and then glide for long distances above the surface.

Red-lipped batfish

This bright-lipped fish is such a poor swimmer that it prefers to use its fins to walk along the ocean floor.

Puffer fish

A puffer fish can inflate to more than double its own size so that it's nearly impossible for predators to eat it.

Frogfish

Frogfish get their name from the shape of their front fins, which bend like frog legs.

JELLYFISH

stinging tentacles

Did you know?

Jellyfish don't have blood, brains, or hearts...and are mostly made of water!

Jelly-fish-saurus

Jellyfish have been around for hundreds of millions of years – that makes them older than the dinosaurs!

CRABS AND CRUSTACEANS

Red king crab

These large crabs have spikes on their outer skeleton to help protect them from predators.

Fiddler crab

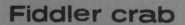

The male fiddler crab has one enlarged claw that can be longer than twice its body width!

Hermit crab

Hermit crabs find protection for their soft bodies from abandoned shells in the sea and carry these around with them.

Did you know?

As hermit crabs grow, they change the shell they carry around to find a larger one.

JAPANESE
SPIDER CRAB

orange with
white spots

strong claws

largest leg span of all crabs

skeleton on the outside

Clever camouflage

This resourceful creature decorates its bumpy shell with sea sponges and other animals to hide itself from predators.

BROADNOSE SEVENGILL SHARK

seven gill slits

Length:

up to 10 ft (3 m)

spotted skin

short snout

wide mouth

Seven is the
biggest number

The broadnose sevengill shark gets its
name from having seven pairs of gill slits.
Most other sharks only have five pairs.

83

QUIZ TIME

1 HOW HEAVY IS A THRESHER SHARK?

.... lbs

2 A THRESHER SHARK CAN WHIP ITS TAIL AS FAST AS 300 MPH (482 KM/H).

true ☐   false ☐

3 JELLYFISH HAVE...

bones. ☐

eyes. ☐

tentacles. ☐

4 WHAT TYPE OF FISH IS THIS?

....

5 THE BROADNOSE

....

SHARK HAS SEVEN PAIRS OF GILL SLITS.

6 WHICH FISH PREFERS TO USE ITS FINS TO WALK ALONG THE OCEAN FLOOR?

puffer fish ☐

flying fish ☐

red-lipped batfish ☐

7 WHAT DOES A WOBBEGONG EAT?

crabs ☐

seaweed ☐

great white sharks ☐

8 CAN YOU RECOGNIZE WHICH ANIMAL HAS BEEN PIXELATED?

....

SHORTFIN MAKO SHARK

The shortfin mako shark is the **FASTEST SHARK** in the sea.

WHERE CAN YOU FIND THEM?

Arctic

North Atlantic

North Pacific

South Pacific

Indian

South Atlantic

WHAT DO THEY EAT?

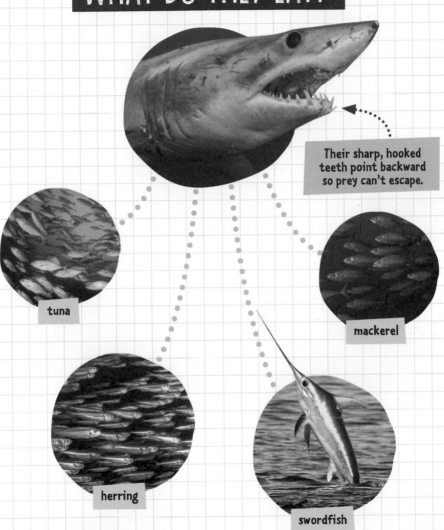

Their sharp, hooked teeth point backward so prey can't escape.

tuna

mackerel

herring

swordfish

HOW DOES THE SHORTFIN MAKO GO SO FAST?

powerful tail

streamlined body

Weight:

up to 1,200 lbs (545 kg)

shortfin mako shark

horse

up to 13 ft (4 m)

pointed nose ·········

Super speed

The shortfin mako shark can swim in short bursts of up to 35 mph (56 km/h). That's nearly as fast as a gazelle running on land!

SAILFISH

The sailfish has a **UNIQUE** sail-like fin on its back that gives it its name.

WHERE CAN YOU FIND THEM?

Arctic

North Atlantic

North Pacific

South Pacific

Indian

South Atlantic

The sailfish is the fastest fish in the sea and can swim up to 68 mph (109 km/h). That's as fast as a cheetah running!

Greenland shark – 1.5 mph (2.4 km/h)

Whale shark – 3 mph (4.8 km/h)

Great white shark – 25 mph (40 km/h)

Octopus – 25 mph (40 km/h)

Shortfin mako shark – 35 mph (56 km/h)

Cheetah – 68 mph (109 km/h)

Sailfish – 68 mph (109 km/h)

WHAT DOES A SAILFISH USE ITS SAIL FOR?

long, sharp bill

Length:

up to 10 ft (3 m)

sail fin

streamlined body

Sailing through

Sailfish usually swim with their sail-like fin folded down. They raise it for swimming at the surface, herding prey, or appearing bigger to predators.

GREAT BARRACUDA

slender body

small scales

Length:

up to 6 ft (1.8 m)

large, sharp
teeth

longer
lower jaw

Fierce predator

These fast predators can attack at speeds
of 36 mph (58 km/h). Their curved,
sharp teeth trap slippery fish.

CORAL REEF

Length:

up to 12 in. (30 cm)

polyp

hard, protective
skeleton at the base

A closer look

Coral polyps can extend their stinging tentacles at night to feed.

tentacles

colony

What is coral?

Coral polyps are simple, soft-bodied creatures. They can live on their own or in colonies attached to rocks on the seafloor.

ZEBRA SHARK

whisker-like barbels
for sensing prey

brown spots

Length:

up to 8 ft (2.4 m)

flexible body

long tail

Spots and stripes

Zebra shark pups have stripes to disguise themselves as sea snakes, but adults are spotted – not like zebras at all!

ANGEL SHARK

These flat, patterned sharks are masters of CAMOUFLAGE.

WHERE CAN YOU FIND THEM?

Arctic

North Atlantic

North Pacific

South Pacific

Indian

South Atlantic

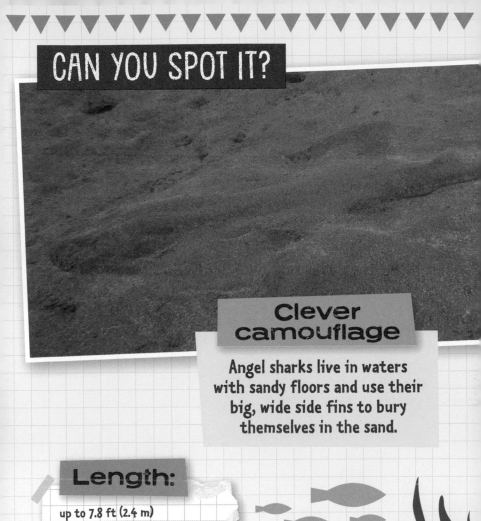

CAN YOU SPOT IT?

Clever camouflage

Angel sharks live in waters with sandy floors and use their big, wide side fins to bury themselves in the sand.

Length:

up to 7.8 ft (2.4 m)

SWELL SHARK

glowing skin

Glow with the flow

Swell sharks absorb moonlight, which makes their skin glow. They use this glow to communicate with others of their kind.

Swelling

When in danger, these sharks swallow water and "swell" to twice their normal size. They also wedge themselves into rocks, where predators can't reach them.

OCTOPUS

An octopus is a soft-bodied animal with eight arms. Its arms are covered in hundreds of sensory suckers. It also has three hearts and no bones!

Lost limbs

Octopuses can regrow arms (including the suckers)!

Clever camouflage

Octopuses can change color and even texture to blend into their surroundings.

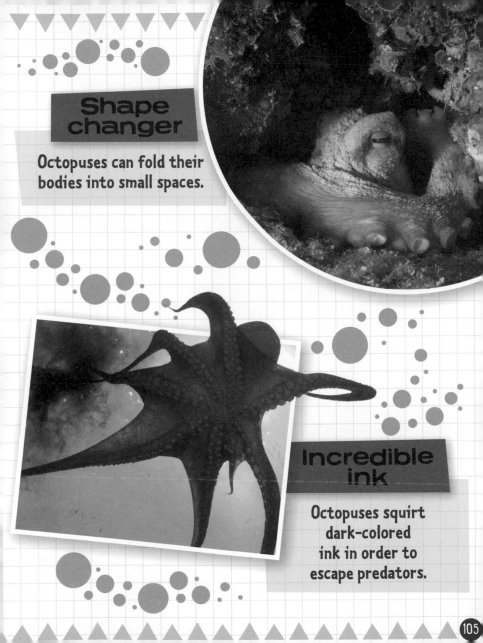

Shape changer

Octopuses can fold their bodies into small spaces.

Incredible ink

Octopuses squirt dark-colored ink in order to escape predators.

QUIZ TIME

1 HOW MANY BONES DOES AN OCTOPUS HAVE?

....

2 HOW FAST CAN A SAILFISH SWIM?

Up to 68 mph
(109 km/h) ☐

Up to 680 mph
(1,100 km/h) ☐

Up to 100 mph
(160 km/h) ☐

3 CORAL POLYPS LIVE TOGETHER IN A COLONY.

true ☐   false ☐

4 SWELL SHARKS CAN SWELL TO...

twice their
normal size. ☐

ten times their
normal size. ☐

three times their
normal size. ☐

5 WHAT TYPE OF FISH IS THIS?

....

6 ....

USUALLY SWIM WITH THEIR SAILS FOLDED DOWN.

7 WHICH SHARK CAN ABSORB MOONLIGHT?

angel shark ☐

tiger shark ☐

swell shark ☐

8 CAN YOU RECOGNIZE WHICH ANIMAL HAS BEEN PIXELATED?

....

BLUE SHARK

pointed nose

big eyes

Length:

up to 13 ft (3.8 m)

metallic
blue skin

sleek body shape

white belly

Long-distance travelers

In search of food and mates, some blue sharks travel from North America all the way to Europe – and back again!

LEMON SHARK

yellow-brown skin

Length:

up to 11 ft (3.4 m)

small eyes

electric sensors

flat, wide head

triangular teeth

powerful tail

Pup protection

Lemon sharks travel to shallow mangroves to give birth. This gives their pups the best chance of survival as they can hide among mangrove roots.

NURSE SHARK

Weight:

up to 263 lbs (119 kg)

nurse shark ▲ reindeer

flat body

gray-brown skin

large barbels

Length:

up to 10 ft (3 m)

small mouth with
vacuum suction

Sociable sharks

A very sociable shark, the nurse shark
sleeps in large groups during the day
and then goes out hunting at night.

WHITETIP REEF
SHARK

Home, sweet home

Whitetip reef sharks live in coral reefs, which are full of 4,000 different fish, crustaceans, and octopuses for them to feast on.

Dinnertime

For their dinner, they use strong sensors and sensitive noses to search out fish that are hiding in among the coral.

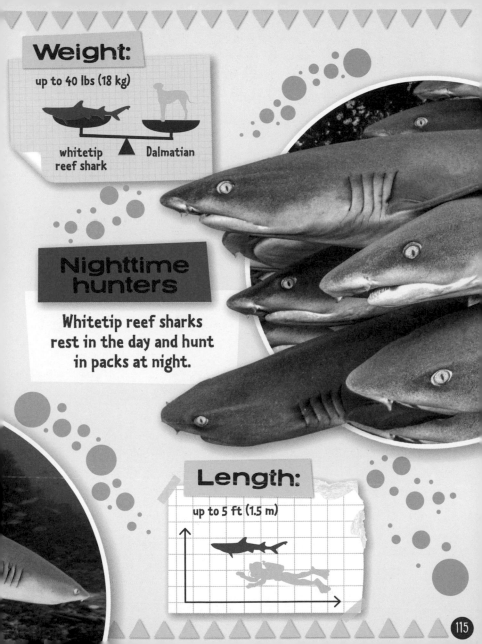

Weight:

up to 40 lbs (18 kg)

whitetip reef shark — Dalmatian

Nighttime hunters

Whitetip reef sharks rest in the day and hunt in packs at night.

Length:

up to 5 ft (1.5 m)

BLACKTIP REEF
SHARK

> The blacktip reef shark is named for the black tips on its fins.

WHERE CAN YOU FIND THEM?

Arctic

North Atlantic

North Pacific

South Pacific

Indian

South Atlantic

WHAT DO THEY EAT?

surgeonfish

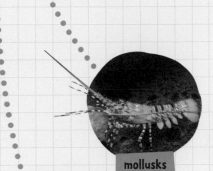
mollusks

wrasses

crustaceans

Weight:

up to 30 lbs (14 kg)

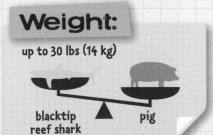

blacktip reef shark | pig

Length:

up to 5 ft (1.5 m)

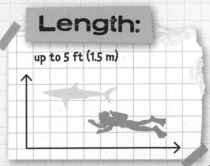

GREENLAND
SHARK

Ancient fish

These slow, gentle giants can live for up to 400 years!

Length:

up to 21 ft (6.4 m)

skin poisonous to humans

In the deep

The Greenland shark is rarely seen by humans because it travels far down to the depths of the ocean, where only robotic submarines can reach.

MEGALODON

Megalodon was a GIANT predator that lived in prehistoric oceans and seas.

sailfish

megalodon

great white shark

jellyfi:

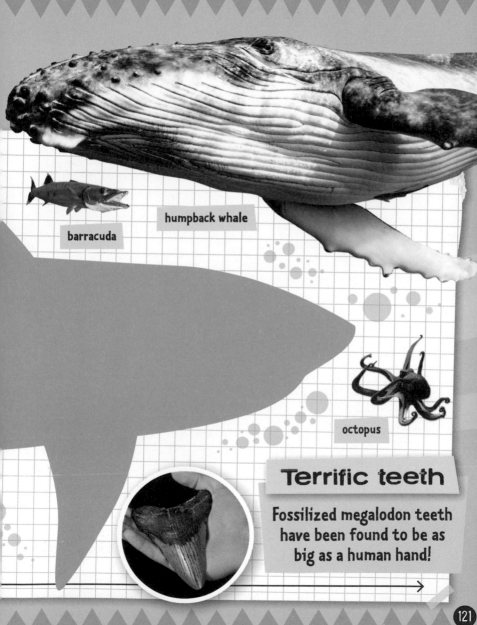

barracuda

humpback whale

octopus

Terrific teeth

Fossilized megalodon teeth have been found to be as big as a human hand!

121

QUIZ TIME

1 HOW MUCH DOES A BLACKTIP REEF SHARK WEIGH?

.... lbs

2 WHITETIP REEF SHARKS HUNT IN PACKS IN THE DAY.

true ☐

false ☐

3 ADULT ZEBRA SHARKS HAVE...

stripes. ☐

spots. ☐

multicolored skin. ☐

4 WHAT TYPE OF SHARK IS THIS?

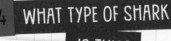

....

5 ....

WAS A GIANT PREDATOR
THAT LIVED IN PREHISTORIC TIMES.

6 HOW LONG CAN A GREENLAND SHARK LIVE FOR?

Up to
1,000 years ☐

Up to
400 years ☐

Up to
50 years ☐

7 WHICH IS THE
LARGEST RAY?

eagle ray ☐

giant
manta ray ☐

blue-spotted stingray ☐

8 CAN YOU RECOGNIZE
WHICH ANIMAL
HAS BEEN PIXELATED?

....

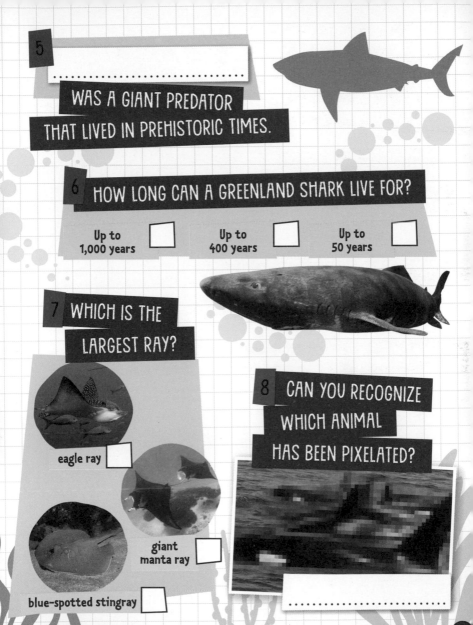

PAGES 22-23

1 A baby shark is called a **pup.**

2 **It's true!** Baby sharks are born with teeth.

3 Great white sharks don't eat **hamburgers.**

4 This is a **tiger shark.**

5 When a great white shark launches itself out of the water, it is known as **breaching.**

6 A great white shark's tooth is bigger than **your ear.**

7 A tiger shark weighs **1,400 lbs (635 kg).**

8 This is a **turtle.**

1 A bull shark weighs **500 lbs (225 kg).**

2 **Muscular jaws** give a bull shark its powerful bite.

3 **It's false!** Bull sharks have poor eyesight.

4 **Gills** enable an eel to breathe underwater.

5 This is a **moray eel.**

6 Moray eels have **two** sets of jaws that help them to bite and swallow large prey.

7 Bull sharks can store **salt** in their bodies.

8 This is a **sea snake.**

1 A whale shark weighs **41,200 lbs (18,700 kg).**

2 The **blue whale** is the largest animal on Earth.

3 **It's true!** Whale sharks are filter feeders.

4 A **beluga whale** can swim backward.

5 This is a **basking shark.**

6 Whale sharks have around 3,000 tiny **teeth**.

7 An orca doesn't eat **humans.**

8 This is a **humpback whale.**

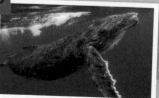

1 A hammerhead shark weighs **1,000 lbs (450 kg)**.

2 **The great hammerhead** shark is the largest species of hammerhead.

3 **It's false!** Mobula rays can do somersaults.

4 **Spotted eagle rays** use their strong sense of smell to sniff out prey.

5 This is a **giant manta ray**.

6 There are **eight** different types of hammerhead shark.

7 Torpedo rays can produce enough electricity to power a **TV**.

8 This is a **blue-spotted stingray**.

1 A thresher shark weighs **750 lbs (340 kg)**.

2 **It's false!** A thresher shark can whip its tail as fast as 30 mph (48 km/h).

3 Jellyfish have **tentacles**.

4 This is a **flying fish**.

5 The broadnose **sevengill** shark has seven pairs of gill slits.

6 A **red-lipped batfish** prefers to use its fins to walk along the ocean floor.

7 Wobbegong sharks eat **crabs**.

8 This is a **Japanese spider crab**.

1 An octopus has **zero bones.**

2 A sailfish can swim up to **68 mph (109 km/h).**

3 **It's true!** Coral polyps live together in a colony.

4 Swell sharks can swell to **twice their normal size.**

5 This is a **shortfin mako shark.**

6 **Sailfish** usually swim with their sails folded down.

7 A **swell shark** can absorb moonlight.

8 This is a **great barracuda.**

1 A blacktip reef shark weighs **30 lbs (14 kg).**

2 **It's false!** Whitetip reef sharks hunt in packs at night and sleep during the day.

3 Adult zebra sharks have **spots.**

4 This is a **blue shark.**

5 **Megalodon** was a giant predator that lived in prehistoric times.

6 A Greenland shark can live up to **400 years.**

7 A **giant manta ray** is the largest ray.

8 This is an **orca.**

127

HOW TO PLAY THE SUPER SHARKS CARD GAME:

1 Press out the cards from the back of the book and shuffle them. Deal the cards between the players. Players keep their cards in a pile, facedown.

2 At the start of each turn, every player turns over their top card. One player chooses a category from their top card and reads out the number.

3 The other players read out the number on their top card from the same category.

4 The player with the highest number wins the turn and collects the cards from the other players. The winning player puts those cards facedown, on the bottom of their pile.

5 The winning player chooses the next category, and steps 2-4 are repeated.

6 The player to collect all of the cards, wins!